MW01527736

M/OTHER

M/OTHER

Poems

Clara A. B. Joseph

RESOURCE *Publications* · Eugene, Oregon

M/OTHER

Copyright © 2024 Clara A. B. Joseph. All rights reserved. Except for brief quotations in critical publications or reviews, no part of this book may be reproduced in any manner without prior written permission from the publisher. Write: Permissions, Wipf and Stock Publishers, 199 W. 8th Ave., Suite 3, Eugene, OR 97401.

Resource Publications
An Imprint of Wipf and Stock Publishers
199 W. 8th Ave., Suite 3
Eugene, OR 97401

www.wipfandstock.com

PAPERBACK ISBN: 979-8-3852-0688-9
HARDCOVER ISBN: 979-8-3852-0689-6
EBOOK ISBN: 979-8-3852-0690-2

VERSION NUMBER 01/24/24

Dedicated to:

The memory of my mother-in-law,
Mariyakutty Varkey Thekkevallyara

*Orpah kissed her mother-in-law goodbye,
but Ruth clung to her.*

—Ruth 1:14 NRSVue

Contents

Freedom

Acknowledgements

The research investigating the philosophical, religious, and postcolonial dimensions that underpin this collection was made possible through funding from a Social Sciences and Humanities Research Council (SSHRC) Insight Grant.

"RESIL(I)ENCE" *You are a flower growing on the side of a cliff.* Ed. Rayanne Haines. League of Canadian Poets, 2021. Revised in this version.

"The Birthday Gift." *RCLAS E-Zine.* [ISSN 2291-4269]. September 2017. Republished in RCLAS 50th Issue of Wordplay at Work. Revised in this version.

"Really Ripe Mangoes." *RCLAS E-Zine.* [ISSN 2291-4269]. September 2017.

"Grandma's Recipe for Omelets." *S/tick* 3.4 (2017) 6.

"Hardboiled Egg." *Canadian Woman Studies* 31.1-2 (2016–17) 64.

"Interruption: An Evening Prayer." *Please Don't Interrupt.* Eds. Rona Altrows and Uchechukwu Umezurike. University of Alberta Press (forthcoming).

Introductions

Are you who you say you are?

body

her eagle-clutch is on my wrist
her vision is lost to mist
but then it arrows
on a stranger

soul

doubt shadows
light fleets recognition
the moon un-reveals
what is far away and the hypocrite
awaits the commissioner-of-oath's query

Meat, Coir, and Metal: A Biography of We

Kitchen appliances hum lullabies and her favorite
soaks in ashen pepper:

Not jowl bacon,
neck chops,
shoulder blade,
diced fatback,
loin chops, or
spare ribs; but

pork, stubborn-whole and slow-
curried in seven condiments
secret.

By their tunnels
MARIA grabs your nostrils,
swings you around,
drowns you in
drool.

***

Before her ancient being
her daughters ran freely
without fouling,
without kinking:

faked down
at every turn
of the looped
tether.

***

Tomorrow?

She will be
full of spark and sulphuric
acid; fool's gold:
pyrite.

Metallic, unwilling
diffusion, she will mirror
the aspect of our dissatisfaction.

Her eyebrow will be
a nickel diacritic:
an up-side-down we.

Mother: A Bio

Outpacing siblings she flung her head
back to laugh, to restart the lightning across
rivers and hills, forests and rice-fields—
commodious spaces.

There was a fever,
there was recovery,
there was a soiled frock, and buttons
undone between short braids on a level back.

Two little eyes took in lessons.

Breasts. Blossoming buttocks.
Curious cousins left behind breath figures;
she traced the frisson with a single braid
fist-thick and knee-level, and in that very place—
the murder of her father.

The darkest substance leaves
indelible roric figures.

One night, she bedded a stranger who came: she became
wife—

dignified
homesick,

spiteful of cloistered nuns,
even of coifs, she drifted

in

out

in

out

in and out
of love
with the same man.

Above the laundry tub again and again
drooped the swollen belly. Three buried

in the backyard (hush! The leaves transpire blood). Six
decreed the objects of her life:
eared notebooks,
stomach-ache cures,
expanding lunchboxes, chewed
pencils,
diarrhea-pills,

ink-stained uniforms, two love-letters,
ballpoints,
and railway tickets. In the stained-glass attic she lay down
for him.

(Will he ascend to heaven, O Lord?)

The widow of Nain wept for her resurrected sons
until they got hitched (alas!). Wedged between
the widow and the wife,
each son wished himself all over again
dead. But day-old infants bawled and she

unlocked her nipples and her songs of usefulness.
She oozed oil onto tiny joints and gifted each
a skilled somatic touch. One threw back his head
to remake her throaty laugh. He grew up
straight-backed.

A granddaughter vaporized
with a feckless lover, gifting her
a heart-attack that she survived
upright.

A son served her
peppered pork, squashed suspicion
with secrets; when she sat back to burp,
he slid her the hidden pen
she admired, then

she signed to him
her widow's fortune—so small,
he demoted her to rice-gruel.

On gruel and anti-depressants her pith grew
plump first, then gaunt, and she began to
bend.

***

she lures

air into a rattling chest beneath
flattering polyester parrot-green.
Red corpuscles starved of oxygen rust her mind:
she can forgive.

How to give
breath?

Jasmine

Palm-perfect planet,
jasmine, queen of night.
Paradise. *Will Pinky*
pick a peck of pretty?
Under the blinking tube-
light she embraced the stars. In the warmth
of her smile they blossomed. Long-
distance. She stretched beyond
the perfumed verandah lines for jasmine
fragrance and restraint. There
for eager rodents and a woman
awaited snakes.

Medullary Carcinoma

Looked in the lake
to the girl there, the lift and mound—
towel tied high. She rippled
into the descent. Unseen. Unfelt.
Bathed, she closed the trap door,
stripped before the mirror, and waited
the pectoral throb. The heat and fever
of bounce and high plump dreamed,
she wrapped like a gift. Unwrapped,
she raced a marathon with a man; his eyes
were shuttered. She watched suckling babes
fattened and leave after
the ablactation
fight.

Looked in the mirror
to the woman there, where the linen
in the inframammary fold hugged
breast to chest, bruising bruise. (Bare-breasted
men strutted like robins.) She removed it
to hidden air. There was a time
when men were kind to some:
Lowly women went upward-
naked or else were taxed
the *mulakkaram*. This one first
then that one she raised for bare.
The place of her shame is still
her pain.

My mother-in-law

was the archetype of a mother
she couldn't grasp, though she
moved through life without murdering;
she conceived: bringing forth sons
and daughters;

she mothered:
                           smothered
vendors and milched her own
mother for more, *more* more;

over real, even imagined, want
her blood broke sweat, and she chuffed
at encircling tantrums.
Her daily living.

In sleep
her doggy-eye alive to un-
shut, her pups latching on to her
glands, she
                           never let go,

until she became
disorganized nursing
this one a little bit more,

cuddling another
a little bit less, day-

by-day, and the honeyed,
green-eyed tyke ruling
reality, blighting

her naïve sister,
and their mother
damning
the un-honeyed tantrums

another forty years thence.
We settled down
to watch
King Lear.

Riding with Mother-in-law

After the six a.m. Mass, mother heads me
to the auto-rickshaw
stand of drivers
dozing and lowered canvas.

In these parts, an early bird is
a crow working
a banana
peel.

A street dog perks up for me and I
for him, then turn away because
the other half-
cares.

The odd tea-shop is open—
straggling widowers
or ones who hope
they will soon be.

I ease in and mother
after me; he shocks
the engine. The seat is tight-
leathered, cool as

steel, and butt to seat
is settling in. He veers
and mother hangs

by the leather loop,
I the damp bar. Shuttered
shops and shop

windows and the art
of merchandise:
Plastic damsels

in bras await
dark shoppers.
Mother asks,

did you pray well?
The conversation is
touch-and-go. My beloved
was fast asleep

and we left for church. It's been three
days since the wedding. Over

once-upon-a-time tarred
roads, the auto goes
rickety rick and I am
fully awake. Thin as a bamboo

she stood,
bloated in one part, looking
fifteen, and I

wonder aloud at her appearance so early

in life. The driver spurts a short
laugh,
speeds.

Everything is normal:
The six a.m. Mass,
mother
stand,
drivers,
canvas,
crow,
banana peel,
street dog,
me,
tea-shop,
widowers,
engine,
seat,
butt,
loop,
bar,
shutters,
shops,
merchandise,
plastic damsels,
bras,
dark shoppers,
conversation,
beloved,
church,
wedding,
days,
roads,
auto-rickshaw,
fifteen-year old,
womb,
driver,
laugh . . . .

Everything is normal
in passing by.

From a Girl of Malabar

Baudelaire, the poet, a bombastic lyricist of the unknown
went to the Mauritius and Réunion to write of India:
    "To a Girl of Malabar."

His girl begets "humming-birds" and "flowers" in "floating dreams"
        at night
after lighting the master's pipe and shopping all day on bare feet.

Pourquoi my foot! He had the nerve to ask:
"Why, happy child, do you want to see our France?"
    Once in Canada,

my mother-in-law slipped into Sorel Nakiska size eight
while her son hopelessly foraged the dank basement for
        my only other pair

in the spirit of taking care. Ridiculously happy, he stole a kiss
every now and then, humping against my tightening front.
    After supper

she unroofed her maxilla into the transparent polidented cup
and all night long the utensil grinned a sunken half grin.

I recently found a still-intact daguerreotype of *her*
        grandparents-in-law,
complete with cigar pipe and unshod feet. The feet were hers

(that much I'll grant Baudelaire); his were booted.
Her eyebrows were stippled well. The young gentleman wore a coat;

he held a cane. The family joke is—when she broke his
    colonial stick,
with the look of a jilted pup, he absquatulated.

And, in a treasured album, a photo of *her* arrival:
the widow of Malabar weeping on her son's neck at
    Toronto Pearson.

It had taken her a while to extricate, to explore the foundling
she once was glad he'd married, procured passport, "visa'd."

There is no art in stating the fact, but Daguerre was
    (to quote Baudelaire)
"a sun-worshipper," Baudelaire an artist, and I—married.

Baudelaire did not like Daguerre.
Just then I liked neither.

(Could I be a Ruth to my Naomi?
Or would I be—simply—ruthless?)

Her look said I was copacetic: there was
no sign of little feet,

my hips hadn't broadened, nor my stomach
distended, but I looked in . . . order.

I am of the same Malabar stock, though
my computer-dulled eyes may not convince the poet.

She on the other hand possessed Baudelaire's "velvety eyes"
    even then;
only, her brown skin was tarnished by the cigarette

stub pressed (with delight) by her master here and there,
here and there. One day she lifted her *sari* to display his cruelty.

This one was for when she had delayed giving him a son,
the one I had married. *His* mother had begun chanting for

a second bride, and my mother-in-law prayed with flooded eyes.
Her velvety ones now rested on me: pray, she instructed.

Sweep and pray.
Weep and pray.

"*Pourquoi, l'heureuse enfant, veux-tu voir notre France?*"
If you really care to know, M. Baudelaire:

after a day of lighting the master's pipe on naked feet
a girl of Malabar is ready to break a stick, to do a bunk.

Falling in Love

That's easy.
In the heart you take a hummingbird's forty-plus beats
a second, in the mind a lifetime of looking
elsewhere—
and soar like an albatross.

Where there was the brine and grind of day
against drag and weight, now
the thrust.

Where there was sweep,
sweep, of spirit and porch
always one gasp behind,
you take the headwind

in your beak
or run
         atop water,
              take off.

Where there were tagged trajectories of space,
now the one channel of your flight,
whose confines are the songs of your salvation,

        desire
              (m)other-bound.

Grandma's Recipe for Omelets

Send little Govind to purchase goatmeat—
Let him walk; he's across the road—the butcher.

Oh, lend him the bicycle! He's stubborn.
His mother was too. Ungrateful *thing*! Got pregnant

at thirteen—a ball upon a twig! By her foster father.
Dirty people! He was a good worker,

though. You could see his bare back from here,
bending over tapioca saplings; and he'd fetch me

curry leaves. I'd call out through this window. See?
Curry leaves refuse to grow these days.

Cucumber leaves will do, to season,
with mustard, chopped onions, garlic,

ginger, green chilies and—come close—
star anise and black pepper. He said he knew

there must be a secret to my curry.
The aroma remained all night and the next morning

upon him. Star anise and black pepper.
A slim, slow stream. It travelled down the middle of

his chest. You will see what I mean. You are old enough to know
how to cook. Crush cinnamon, cardamom, and of course some

cloves. Grind chili, turmeric, and coriander into paste.
Oh! You have all these as powder. Chili powder! Turmeric powder!

Coriander powder! Ha! Life is easy for you. Listen!
These get burnt too quickly!

She tried to commit suicide. Twice. This is his son.
He's not back as yet? It'll be omelets tonight.

On Felicitating Her Son for a Poem Published

Celebrations are explosives, firecrackers, requests for purchase
    and pound,
or boom or boom boom boom startling monsoon's rest and
    the rising moon.
Somewhere there is water to whet aspirations in its tiding,
    mists, and microbes,
in sweet-stuffed puffs, jamun swims, and the breached biriyani.
    I am a telltale,
tail tucked in and horns hair-wound. Mother is in the kitchen,
    crawling.
A goat kid strays or sprays droppings in the back porch and
    I become
conversant with the floor. Dust is only tedious others gone to rest.
To hell with it! At least my back is worth a gamble when discs take
the shock. The germs under my claws, like the confidence
    of squatters
who brush off their pockets, like their kids, claim God's space.
    There are some
winners. She thinks we ought to arrange for fireworks—poppers
    at least.
Wherever her sons are, there is no need for purchased bangs
    and booms,
I fume. Her laughter is hale-and-hearty, like she is proud or what,
like she thinks she'll catch his sight even at his height.

On Putting the Fear of God in Me

A woman bends in prayer,
a.k.a., sweeps the compound;

she leaves behind a testimony—
a.k.a., broom-marks, after sprinkling

the dust to rest. A woman
wakes up at four. One by one

a woman drops the jaggery balls,
she prays (again) with the church bells

rising from the pot; she fills the cup
for the hibernating male still on their cot.

A woman . . . .

A woman . . . .

No compounds to sweep;
not even jaggery in Canada,
I declare. Best of all,
no wake-up call at four. He fondles

the long-distance phone
after vacuuming that first time; soon enough
Mother gives *me* her (Telus) catechism:

You should know
at least to vacuum
when angels unroll
God's red carpet.

From Under the Transcendental Carpet

After the offending floor was stripped
leaving two inches of soft dust

out crawled ants
from the earth, balancing

specks of sticky red, wondering
which way God went.

Her Gospel

The Birthday Gift

We celebrate her birthday with paper
at our convenience. There is no date in her stone age.
To be fair, we were never there
on her unknown birthday affair.

From a past Christmas, we pick paper chains,
origami, and snowflakes; then the excuse of sons:
The day Mother was born,
we weren't there haha.

She is lost to doze and babble, and we are
senseless. I take over the kitchen
space for chicken biriyani, cutlets,
oven-baked kingfish, and onion
salad—off the restaurant chef. Before

three generations arrive with giggles,
whining, and chatter, I snatch a patch on her lap
careful not to let go of the burden

of my head. I can tell
she likes it in her ruffle of my hairdo.
There is no one else in her sight.

She leans back.
She closes her eyes.
        There is nothing.

She has never sat back quite like that,
and I wasn't pressing her against
the settee or
her will.
She is leaning back,
closing her eyes, resting

in life.
As I raise my head
for confirmation, she tells me: I remember

your father. Medication has brought this on,
surely! *My darling Father died only yesterday.*
Only twenty-five years ago.
I remember being at his funeral, she says, eyes closed like a joke.
He was in the military, she says. I remember.

And as I raise my head to look at her,
she tells me again: I remember.

Raw on my nerve is her secret.

Blut ist dicker als Wasser?

Of all our private relations, blood is the most intense, carrying care one way, greed the other way. But, in the cavern of our conscience, we find a drop, which we have not loaded up ourselves, which we must heed as on our visits across the seven seas.

Of all our private relations, *they* refused to dislodge: St. George's dragon neatly doubled to stop access, one on her right and the other on her left, or like Christ's thieves—one not so clueless and the other snatching paradise. I say blood is thicker than all seven seas. Stench of dragon tails and flames; approach repelled: blood rose at high tide and I, not blood, withdrew. It was then she beckoned me, not behind their backs. She was upfront. She drew the spirit, which first limped then found footing and raced to us finally.

Of all our private relations, we began to hear Mother speak and so we listened to ourselves. Interiority.

The Epistle of MARIA

On the kitchen counter, tomatoes, Rosie,
and the other men
you fancied.

There is bite-sized air to
wish a birthday:

no honey. Let's make love
to a plough

when we retire.
I spread the wrapper
like a shroud
of the Nothing

that I purchased
like a wife.

I am
impaled

on the spokes of your work,
the re-invented wheel.
You are busy

is the sound
of your breath.

Relatives make
tin-laughter
with our food,
and nights beg—begin anywhere.

Nights:
listening to you

snore. Up,
all men are nightmares—palms drip like widows.

Behold
harvest.

Interruption: An Evening Prayer

May the Lord
Coop the chickens!
Bless you! And keep you!
May the Lord let
him die alone, won't you?!
Now where was I?! Yes—
His face shine upon you
And for goodness sake! *Be gracious*
to you! May the Lord
uncover his face to you
and (my little one sat in his
father's lap like an insult thirty years)
bring you sit up straight or sin-sleep!
Peace! Now you, my grandchild, read!
ThisishowyouaretocalldownmynameonthesonsofIsrae
landIwillblessthemsaystheLordNumbers6:24to26.

Jesus,

Mother, before they lived together, was the Holy Spirit.
Her hus, being a man,
to divorce her quietly resolved
in a dream, and the child
conceived in her.

She will bear a son, and name him,
his people, and their sins.

All is spoken by the prophet:
the virgin shall give birth
and name him man,
which means, God.

Joseph took her
but had no marital relations
until she had given birth to a son.[1]

---

1. Excised from *Matt* 1:18-25 (NRSVue)

Magi

Magi from the East
ask where to pay:
Hen rod priests scribes
people Messiah. They told,
it has been written:
you are the least
for you shepherd
her secretly.

Go and search,
bring and pay the king
her head, the star of the east.

When they saw the star
they were overwhelmed with joy.
Mary knelt,
offered gold.
And they left
by another road.[2]

2. Excised from *Matt* 2: 1-12 (NRSVue)

Escape

Joseph in a dream
said, remain there until
I tell you.

So, Mother by night went
to Egypt and remained
until death to fulfill
what had been spoken:
"Out of Egypt I have called my son."[3]

3. Excised from *Matt* 2: 13-15 (NRSVue)

The Massacre

Her trick infuriated and killed
the children who had learned
from the prophet.

hear
lament
weep

no more[4]

4. Excised from *Matt* 2: 16-18 (NRSVue)

The Return

Her angel appeared to Joseph
and said, "Get up man."

Then Joseph got up,
and went to the land.

He was afraid to go there.
And after being warned,
he went away to the district. There
he made his home in a town.
He will be called.[5]

---

5. Excised from *Matt* 2: 19-23 (NRSVue)

The Spoilt Growth

In Mother's courtyard stood a nameless tree
whose fruit none of us fondled
for it grew
slant.

Ten little children ringed
its massive trunk. But the reckless
branches sprang elsewhere,
where scoundrels plied stones
all day and battled with the bees. Now and then
a stone-bruised neighbor

appeared before Mother promising
vengeance. In her tongue Mother declared,
make my day. And the other went
away and swore, and did—
nothing. It was too late
to prune. Mother insisted
the tree unbend.

We've caught her grazing
by the turned-away tree. We've seen
her in slow ritual,
circling once, circling twice,
then one more pleading time,
touch the trunk, like tenderness,
then leave. If you believe

a toothless servant's rant,
she's circled all her merry married
life: "You'd think it sprouted
in her womb."

One day, the electricity boss arrived and spat
on her creation: Its lowly twigs grazed the sacred public
wires. Silence stoned him. But the next day

she laid the axe
at its root.

The chips flew
as she struck
her breast for
hours on end.
Servants resolved
the job. Who cut whom?
If Lazarus should die,
why would God cry? Her pith
to heartwood, she fondles
the wound of the stump.
In its medullary rays she reads
hieroglyphics and turns
grim. Her vision is
our caution: As if

to meet her child
or God, Mother stands
axe in hand.

Why No Easter Breakfast this Year

The day Lot left behind his lot, cabbages morphed purple.
Then each burst into a cluster of fire and sulphur
with caps and exclamation marks. Lotswife turned
for one last look (at her cabbages) and hardened into salt.
She for one never renounced
her saltiness.

Now you just answer me: how can it be "*like that*
on the day that the Son of Man is revealed"?
John. He came later than Luke. First Luke.
Luke said: "Remember Lot's wife." What he meant was:
She was a you-know-what or cabbage-looker.
So, John, who had a troublesome mother, wanted
another (he was, you see, a mother-collector);
he plucked off the Lord's robe and wound
around him a towel instead. Between Luke (and his sort)
and John, the Lord pedicured twelve,
without a scissor,
clean of the day's pickerel catch.

Lotswife began to toboggan
the Lord's fortune: Gethsemane to Golgotha. Gethsemane
ensorcelled the drunken crowd to sweet slumber
while the Lord stood pleading to them for company
at age thirty-three. Even John was still
snoring in the garden
when Luke referred to an angel in velour—
a comfort. Whereupon the Lord sweated
great drops of blood to the ground. Golgotha

after the gnathic slap and the cheek turn, turn,
turn, and turn again and again; after the crow,
after the crow of the cock, after the cock crow
(that's one, two, three to be exact); after all are awake:
the slapper fumbles for an answer and teary-eyed-Peter becomes
a gorge of salt-water serpentine,
later, across continents.

The motley crowds weave their way to Golgotha
where the blackened ground is once again reddened,
where John stands expectant before
the King of Lotswife.

That was nine a.m. Six hours later,
John bags the Lord's mother:
the Lord dies,
the curtain tears,
the earth shakes, the saints topple
out of their tombs, the Lord is
entombed, then promptly
un-tombed.

Lotswife and I?
We take the day off.

On Reconciling God and Man

In the stir of a grey exam,
as if the devastated sleep was petering out,
slumber's silence met the dawn,
when a word then another made too much
sense and the coherence of her speech was
just too much, a bothered crowd flocked
around her bed. Her eyes were shut.
She looked pleased and her lips
were sealed when the immovable ceiling
began to speak. We checked
the flat innocence and spied
a fat lizard lisping a hypnotized fly:

not a morsel would she eat
until her grandson returned
well past his third attempt
on a fated test, for God had commanded
her thus. The ventriloquist was serious.
So, we Amened, then crawled
right back into our abandoned beds.

Breakfast came and went,
the candidate, powdered and dressed, had long left,
but God's voice kept falling off the roof.

At noon, I encountered her God with mine:
God had just spoken to me—hot off the press—
to save her child she must lunch.

She had her doubts, but bent she was
on reconciling God and the young man.

On my way back to the kitchen sink,
I contemplated the licked plate
and believed in the Atonement.

The Transfiguration

Her alive was once a man,
but today she's widowing:
Hus hus hus hus hus . . . . Flashback

a dripping village. Bathers
are friends querying her man—
mysterious at the edges:

In her own tale, she rises.
He prices her drench and drip,
her plump and press in orchards.

At home she is a salt bitch,
and her parents are deadly.
Made eyes at him till cockcrow.

We tease her now to freeze tears,
yet a trickle trails her cheek:
no tapioca today.

Without him, she will not nick
the dish . . . his fervent lick . . . his
tongue pink . . . . Hus hus hus hus hus . . . .

turned ill like a machete
blow and could prune no more sons
grown unsheared, unwieldy.

(God knows we want him alive,
to shear unwieldy ones.)
We reason how long she'll vex.

Hus hus hus hus hus hus hus . . . .
When Madhavan appears bright
around her corner, we breathe.

His hairy smile is a crow
carrying coconut chip,
and he coos into her plight.

She forecloses the civic
smile, and we signal to him:
Before her hung her framed man.

Then appears the furuncle
wrist held behind all the while—
a flask of golden arrack.

She smiles a dawning sparkle
and prods the native flask of
rum: how do you do today?

Oh, not bad at all today!
He knows knives, jives, and wives; winks
at us—aches were for the swig.

The fluttering brood behind
reigns her in. She twists, turns, feigns
disinterest's long minute.

We ready-steady her cup.
We slide it within her reach.
Madhavan then golds the pour.

From her couch, Mother inhales.
On the floor, squats Madhavan,
granted his clay of comfort.

"*Adi Ammachi!*" he cheers.
And she to him. In single
gulps cups empty themselves at

once. Heads jerk. Shoulders shudder.
The cups return to their rest.
A singular nod approves

zing. She turns to study me
and then looks the other way
the other hinky up-down.

Something hinky's afoot—she
conveys her mind to him, which
look he mimics like Lever.

Mother unscrolls her story,
this time to Johnny Lever.
Wise he sits, drinking . . . hus hus . . .

hus . . . . At the moment we fear
the return of the salt bitch,
she rants of illness and want:

She grew four sons, inch by inch.
She fed them; she fought them; she
found them—four buxom fools.

Shock un-tempts Madhavan's eyes
from assaults of buxomness.
Over our giggles, she wails—

Ayyoooo . . . ayyoooo . . . . The waves rise
and balloon bang. Worried hands
pound an open door and push.

The code is, "Madhavan's here."
She roars again—for the shot;
the two pick up—eager cups.

"*Adi Ammachi!*" She drawls—
each girl by her christened name.
She peers, divines we're scared:

it is only her: M . . . other.
Madhavan sparks it, spelling—
we've all peed in pajamas.

She laughs laughs her free minutes,
to which arrives the third cup,
galvanizing our futures:

No one shall depart again.
Never apart shall we live.
She taps her cup to locate—

there exactly we will live
happily ever after.
We've been through *this*, we've been *through*

this. Many, many times we've
watched the tragedy unfurl;
each time she messed-up sons' good-

byes. Yet bright now, self-possessed,
her dreams ballooning in booze,
she'll raise four stories for her

four; they will visit by day,
they will visit her by night,
they will visit her till death

do us part. Till death *do*
us *part*. Till *death* do us
part . . . . And she begins to snore
to our jagged chant.

on writing "The Transfiguration"

at the death chant
i stare in horror
refusing to look
into the mirror

The Door

Her hair has been axed, and the lice
knocked dead into a bonfire.
She is ready to perceive us,
her face masked fresh
with ashes. Instead,

she blares a secret:
I am a well-known saint.
My name is in the papers.

Ain't I too a saint, Mother?
He greets her good mood.

You? She strikes—
If you stop being a bad boy, you will.

Her palm, man-strong, strikes,
strikes as he binds her,
strikes him hard to ward off
the curse she has
bolted from the inside.

A Broken Slam

Write down everything, she commands
from the hospital bed and I obey
because her body says she's dying,
but she won't just yet, and her eyes
remain fierce and the fire
grows from a spark to a lamp to
a bush. Write everything down
she tells me as she tears
off the oxygen mask,
and I begin to write.
She has woken under sedatives,
ranting—the world, and not her
back, is broken, shattered under
reservations of castes and tribes
as we gained from preservations
of their distress. The world, and not
her back, is broken, when some uncles
shared all night an orphaned teen
who disappeared, then reappeared
as an old mad woman at her back door,
whom she chased away with pennies.
The world is broken she says pointing
to the priest who has arrived to give
healing, when a nun is raped and muffled.
Broken, broken, she cries, broken when
the homily is so boring that congregations
relax when it is all ended
and prayers so distant that little children go nowhere
near Jesus, and the empty church

is not a place for refugees or widows.
Today the world broke, she said, when
the brown nurse joined hands with the white
nurse to starve the bearded black youth
nine hours straight in the Emergency.
She said she was watching
as the boy licked clean
a thimble of Pepto-Bismol.
You could tell he was hungry,
she said. And then she's all silence and I
let my pen rest, but it is only a pause,
for she hurts again. Broken, she weeps,
like hearts when they part
midway or ways or sometimes stay
to make the other pay and the children
shatter like glass; each fragment
repays a thousandfold to parents,
siblings, and all who cross their paths.
The world was broken, she says, when
her father was stabbed in the back by a brother
or a neighbor, "we never were sure," she says,
and he died in the dark, but his land remained
ours, and for that he died. He died, she says, and we told
him and we couldn't hold him,
we told him, we told him,
but we couldn't hold him back
for our sake as we ate the fruit of his hand,
and the land—it soaked with fertilizers and blood.
The world is broken, she says, when fertilizers
make farmland into desert and a young wife,
with a dream and an infant at her breast wakes up
to an empty bed, because her man has taken
his own life to kill a debt, to flee the money-
lenders at his heels; there's no helping hand,
only a long-dead land, and the suicide notes

keep piling, piling, piling up, kept for
generations. Oh, she's hurting,
hurting, and I am writing, writing and I ask
for relief, but her words—they're hurtling
down white pages, and I ask for relief, but her words
keep pouring down my eyes, and I am sniffling
and I need to blow my nose.
Yes, broken, she says, like
a yoke, and I think an egg, but she goes on,
it wasn't a light burden that broke
her mother after she played both father
and mother to thankless lepers—all nine,
after she broke the land into ten and after
she gave hers to them, and after
they threw her into a corner, she died
like a leper, broken by sons.
So I keep writing, writing,
because she says the world
is broken. Broken like a plate!
Broken like the hundreds
of plates she washed and dashed
throughout her life. So, she says,
through the cracks, she says, through
the cracks, the cracks, through the
cracks of brokenness, the broken parents,
the children, she says, and the night:
through the cracks of the broken parents,
even at night the children—
through the cracks—get some light.
Write down everything she commands
from the hospital bed and I obey
because her body says she's dying,
but she won't just yet, and her eyes
remain fierce and the fire
grows from a spark to a lamp to
a bush. And Moses took off his shoes.

A Psalm

I shall not
lie down
beside still waters;
my soul paths
His name sake.
I walk the darkest evil,
for you are rod.
You prepare enemies
with my cup.
Surely mercy shall follow all
and I shall dwell in the house
my whole life.[6]

6. Excised from *Ps* 23, 1-6 (NRSVue)

The Psalm of My Shepherd

The Psalm of my shepherd
makes me lie down,
leads me, stores me for his sake.

Though I walk
I fear
you are with
rod and fort.

Pare my head, my goodness,
and mercy. O my life
in the house.
My life.[7]

---

7. Excised from *Ps* 23, 1-6 (NRSVue)

The Divine

I want green pastures
beside still waters.
My soul, He is the darkest valley;
fear me; staff me; table me
in the presence;
anoint my head with oil.

My cup overflows.
Surely follow me all, and I shall
house the LORD long.[8]

---

8. Excised from *Ps* 23, 1-6 (NRSVue)

Really Ripe Mangoes

At my mother-in-law's
The thud

Thud

Thud

Thud thud

Are mangoes
Ripening to the earth

All day
All night

Self-giving

Freedom

RESIL(I)ENCE

My boy taught you to look at a word,
a different one each time, and leap into
sleep and out like a stallion or a night-
mare:

ervation
olution
erve
ident
idence
ervoir
earch

you pluck the glue: *a particular thing: MATTER —*
(used especially in legal phrases).

He smiled like the man he was
as he copied wonder into my lap,
his notebook steadied at an angle.
And I bent to smell his washed scalp;
the nip was barely visible. The dancer,
he says (he wouldn't say answer),
is (he reads impatience; I pre-
tend; he waits; we await)
res!

I
have nothing to say.
My heart of 1972 is in tatters;

the herd scatters his words.
The arc of their bellow is unremarked:
They formed a circle to mark his place
of rest, and that is how we found him.

And the snake slid away
in the shadows between
our hooves.

Have you ever seen the uncaged bird grow
old and die?

There

I've said it, and perhaps not, not
really, but I have his words like
images. *An image is an image not
because it is not the real. An image is
an image because it reminds me
of the real.* Prosaic
in my mouth, his words are . . . .

(I won't say mine) . . . .
His words,
spine.

Senility

My brother-in-law decides to test
the soundness of his mother's
head. He points at me,
his sister-in-law.

He spreads his words feet apart:

Who

Is

That?

My daughter.

Choosing Senility

I have powdered my face
with chalk,

stuck gulmohar
petals on nails, and reddened

my lips with mulberries.
I have eaten

a stolen egg.
I have desired a baker

for his rows of
cakes,

cookies,
and scones.

I have unbraided
my braids and swirled

a hairdo. I have told
my boys to pick

fallen hair. I have
searched for my glasses

resting on my nose.
I have rolled money

by the penny.
I have kissed

in the attic.
I have mated.

I have wrung his children
drawn from my womb.

I have soaked
the mattress and moved

my bowels
on the mosaic floor.

I have chosen
the time to be deaf.

I have chosen the time
to be blind.

I'll switch it all back on when
I choose.

The Ambiguous Image

Maria (granddaughter)

arranges her favorite things:
rouge,
lipstick,
nail-polish,
slippers and shoes to go
with sarees,
blouses,
jeans,
lingerie.
There are the trips
to the beautician,
the hairstylist, and a change
of earring,
bangles,
purses, and then
the selfies, and then
the selfies.
She has bells
on her toes,
anklets of gold,
a nose stud, etc.
She has belts:
blue, yellow,
green, and black.
You detect
their continuing edges.

MARIA (GRANDMOTHER)

cannot
find her

glasses.
She has an emptying

trunk of clothes
no one else filches,
like
nighties and nighties and nighties with
no underwear.
Her bible
quotes are
tattered.
Water shall clean
face,
mouth,
eye.
She
cannot
find

her teeth for trips
to the clinic.
Her missing

earring,
gold bangles, and a gold

chain she hordes
in a drawer
of her mind. She watches
a movie with eyes

closed and feet
belted.

You detect
Maria, then, MARIA,
or MARIA, then, Maria. You detect
their continuous edges until

the ambiguous image
snuggles.

When a Son Hears His Mother Call

The voice from a distance is the stomach sucked
all the way in, touching the spine. Mother calls

this way for hours on end. Mother calls those dead,
those at work, and those hiding. She tells me

I died; but she ignores me all the same.
She could have easily been

an opera singer, with a voice travelling
past the neighbor's cows—they pause, listen,

hesitate to graze. Even the dog returns
the slipper it stole last night and flees

when Mother takes a short
breath. The mesh tears, the pane

shatters, the rods of iron bend,
and the sill loses its final grip before

I can say: "she's calling." The power
of *yogic* sound! I believe in Genesis!

I believe in Genesis! I dream that night—
Mother is laid to rest, freshened by flowers

sprouting from her coffin. With her head swathed,
but her face exposed, she looks comfortable

inside my mosquito net. Then I hear her
call. This time she calls for me.
Someone is surely dead!

Ninety Years of Modesty

I don't like men kissing me, she says,
as the eldest fills goodbyes with cling and vocabulary.
Shoes shining, a hanky in *each* pocket, wearing
underwear—clean, he promises her;
he shall return intact.

Our last visit from abroad was five years ago,
and she's led to the bath and all

where she is chanting with the eagles
for balm and calm. What are you waiting
to see?! Her child scuttles out of her sight,
having stretched out his care
through the half-open door. I feel shy,

we hear her cry. The nightie!
Quickly!
And it arrives
on eagles' wings as she turns ninety.

Through the Voile

Suddenly you are gone, your face
crumbled silk, your hair grey
knotted thread.

Between the kitchen rag
and the quilt, you wore swan-white. And just this once
I baste you over my mother.

Others dress up for the ritual. I take to your
Singer, to rest my head
against your metal bed, remembering
men and children went about their tattered business
in your mending presence. I stretch you out

like limbs and draw sheer fabric,
white voile, top to toe. In a dream
one sews strange things.

The room empties like a spool
for my future—
the distant tomorrow you once secured
with a pin.

Voiled caution predicts
the situation: the face
traces a poem.

the wound

is a throbbing secret,
raw under
the fresh bandages of her Home.

The hole is big—
the moon of her thumb and forefinger waxes
for family; her eyes narrow

like arteries, and her words stick out
like legs. She might as well be talking
love and heartache—

of un-healing. For bitterness is
silence. Under the bandages,
it is rotten; the limb is threatening

to fall off. We humor her
imagination. The diagnosis is "peripheral
arterial disease."

But to guess what is under,
to guess what is under,
one must linger.

Remembering at Ninety

There she sat—a bright egg
in the haystack a curious child
discovered one holiday.

Luminescent with sudden remembering,
fragile and on the verge of
sobbing,

she will wait for me.
The program ending in ten minutes gnawed
into my obligation, and I arrived in a flutter;
feathers flipped in my path, and she
began to laugh. I raised her lightness;
examined her brightness up close. I

remember now. She could barely talk for
her excitement. When I tried to walk her back,
she jerked away my hand.

She stood me still. Concerned, she checked for
my sanity. She commanded my attention:
nothing to worry about. I

remember now. She was
glittering as she palm-warmed my chin,
trembling.

At my eventual comprehension, she bobbed with
relief, and I waited. I remember,
she began again, her voice cracking, I remember . . .

something.

She Died Three Days Before Christmas

The stand and the trunk and the myriad leaves;
shouts of insanity are from the clutter called
a corridor. The skirt, rustic red-and-black,
awaits the will of man and wife, settles
at weight of stand and trunk, branches
of human engineering and lessons:
long first, not this . . . try another
. . . okay . . . got it . . . where . . . that
goes there . . . you do it . . .
a peck on the cheek;
self-congratulating,
a hug on done.
Gift-boxes
unopened
look

suspect. The lights
taken out twirl the Tannenbaum.
Tall, he lifts an angel for tree-topper.
She squats by the cord for red-sted-go
looking four, frightened at an imaginary
scuttle of garage mice from a past Christmas.
At the awaited signal, she flicks the switch for fiat
lux, and rises. They stand back and are taken aback
by more than electricity: a visitation of loving admiration.
No divinity can surpass this maternal presence and the light
brightens manifold at sheer joy and gasp. Just then the phone rang—

the long-distance
chime from two-
dawns-before-
Christmas
India—and
they wept
for the light.

A Son's Eulogy

A High Mass,
an alarm that went off
in the dark, a black coffee,
the same book,
a ripple laugh,
a tickle on the dawning
pillow, the snarl
at "bad friends,"
the banisher
of card games and bettors,
a sudden lightening
in broad daylight,
a witch.

A slow walk,
rest for the aged
Ambassador hatching;
for the driver,
gardening lessons
more than part-time;
music contrapuntal
in the parish, at home
off-key seven times
seventy, a despair
louder than homework,
a miracle.

A counter of coconuts
quicker than a calculator,
a win-win-pawn-shop,
a canteen for heart and belly,
a meeting hall, a deviser
of the next, a woman
father called "a problem"—
front-teeth smiling,
clench barely hidden;
well after the monsoon,
a drenching storm.

A back
bent to the split,
a banquet for other
people's children;
a crushed red chili
chutney; a double-tongue:
a bitter-truth pill
sweet for the swallow,
self-pity's thrash,
its whimper's
live burial, and when God
went hiding,
a prayer.

A laughter across the valley
paused by mountains.

On her anniversary

Cars, cars, and cars driven to slow;
furtive stray dogs crisscross
with practiced pedestrians,
tracing the outlines of automobile.
Scantly draped in five-feet sarees
the ivory mannequins smile red
at human arrivals. Across the street, fruit
carts. Vodafones recharge conversations.
Life towns.

Back in my room, the mirror nods on a loose hinge:
matches top to bottom, disciplines
unruly hair, and confirms as blended
the clutched purse. She calls

my name from two years ago: engrossed in money-counts,
logic-shouts, and justice-fists, her daughter and I
stared each other down. I was leaving in an hour but
I had forgotten, until she called me by my name,
until she alerted me to the flight
of time and I, falling to my knees
before her fragility, hid my guilt
in her palm.

The money and the logic—
what's more—justice itself have made
their daily rollcall well after
she is gone. Finally, I take the ride
to her. Tears on stone.

An Ear for Music

That's how we've done it these years of listening
the rattle and the chomp chomp timing,
each other baring the split chest through breaking
bones and chewing liver.

That's how we've done birthdays on a
whim and a skim—howls of wolves,
tigers, and the bloody arrogant peacocks with feet
utterly disgusting; so we whip

the crap and br/others; so we fumble
through the crumble—degenerating discs.
The rattle and the rattle

our gifts to our children,
their children, and our well-
practiced bellows
lungs.

A Teardrop

a) A plant you watered has sprouted blighted. Should I blame or bless you?

b) You asked me once and once only, and I said once and once only: nothing doing. Why does it ring a thousand times to wreck my life?

c) I meant to purchase Cuticura talcum powder. I meant.

d) To save you labor I ate out, but forgot to bring home a plate.

e) I banished you from my honeymoon train. We are barren. Because.

f) You said I dressed you up like a queen for a party; but then you cared only for your womb. I remember. I forgive. Which is true? You say the two are one. And then you ask: true?

g) You were upset about my barrenness; so, I kissed your raised palm, and you forgot. I remember. I forgive. The two are one.

h) I fed you pills for thyroid and pressure, but they were really anti-depressants. You remembered.

i) You hold your silence too long for fear of me telling. I can tell.

j) Something I will never ask you: what is it that shines at the rim of a paradox?

Hardboiled Egg

I've never tasted
boiled egg so good
as from your hands
that still morning at ten
when I was just about to leave
and two suitcases stood
large and locked
for the taxi
the knapsack still on my back
holding a face-towel
the poisoned bible
a wallet and a toothbrush
a tube of paste
a tongue-cleaner

you had it ready
unshelled and warm
at the tip of a thumb and two fingers
as if you'd ordered the hen
to lay so well ahead
for you to just pluck
the warmth from the hay
the yoke especially made
for me so smooth
oh so round
even the smell oh
so perfect

it is a pity
just to bite and break
such wholesomeness
and you in that posture

of letting go

Printed in the USA
CPSIA information can be obtained
at www.ICGtesting.com
JSHW012236290224
58210JS00005B/18

9 798385 206889